Skateboarding Skills

Skateboarding
Skills

Ryan Stutt

FIREFLY BOOKS

A FIREFLY BOOK

Published by Firefly Books Ltd. 2014

First printing

Publisher Cataloging-in-Publication Data (U.S.)
A CIP record for this title is available from the Library of Congress

Library and Archives Canada Cataloguing in Publication
A CIP record for this title is available from Library and Archives Canada

Published in the United States by
Firefly Books (U.S.) Inc.
P.O. Box 1338, Ellicott Station
Buffalo, New York 14205

Published in Canada by
Firefly Books Ltd.
50 Staples Avenue, Unit 1
Richmond Hill, Ontario L4B 0A7

Cover and interior design: Kimberley Young
Illustrations: George A. Walker
Trick photographs: Will Jivcoff

Special thanks to CJ's Skateboard Park and School for the use of the skate park for trick photography.

Front Cover Image: iStock/gilltrejos
Back Cover Images: Will Jivcoff

Printed in the United States of America

The publisher gratefully acknowledges the financial support for our publishing program
by the Government of Canada through the Canada Book Fund as administered by
the Department of Canadian Heritage.

Additional Photo Credits
T = top; B = bottom; M = middle; L = left; R = right.

Márk Zádor and Attila Horváth 10R

Shutterstock Images:
Kunertus 18T; Lzf 8R, 11, 28, 92; Marc-Andre 19B; Lukas Majercik 10L; Mskorpion 23–24; Nito 18B; Tim
Roberts Photography 9R, 22; Underworld 12T&M; Konjushenko Vladimir 12B; Nick Witten 8L, 21, 90;
Sergey Yechikov 19T.

Contents

Skateboarding Primer

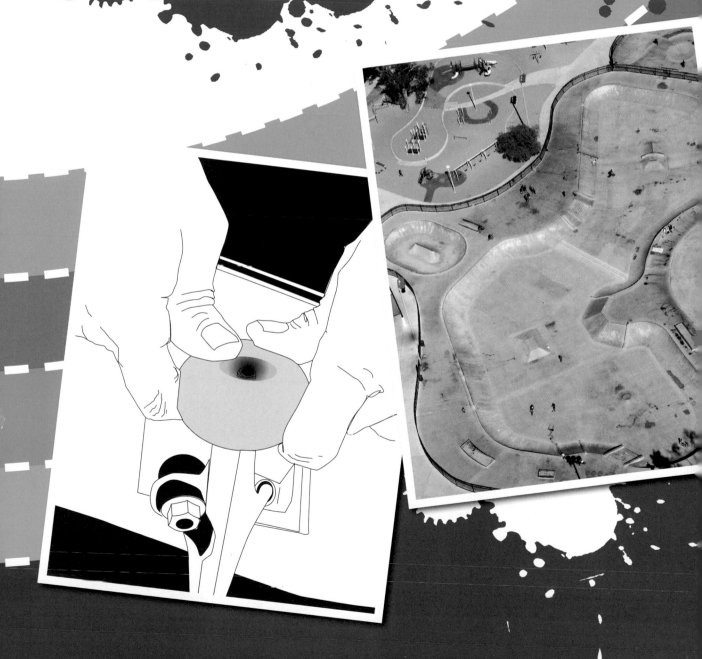

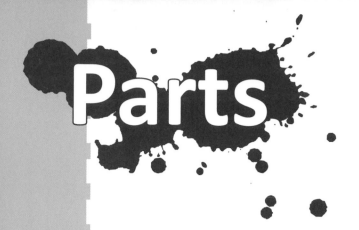

Parts

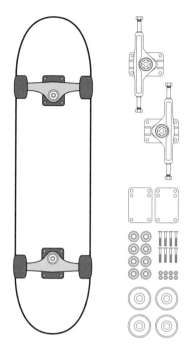

SKATE DECK

Sometimes referred to as a board, the deck is seven layers of wood of the same size and shape that are pressed together with glue so they all stick together. The piece at the bottom is called the bottom sheet, and that is where the graphics are painted. The top sheet is called, you guessed it, the top sheet. Using layers of wood (instead of one solid piece of wood) makes the board more durable and also more flexible.

The layers are molded in such a way that the front and back of the deck are angled upward. The front of the board is called the nose, and the back is called the tail. The deck also curves from the toe side to the heel side, in what's called the concave of your board. This curving gives the rider more control over the deck during tricks. The concave will vary from board to board, so stand on a few different ones to find out which angle you find most comfortable.

Most street skateboards are between 7 and 8¼ inches (17.75–21 cm) wide. Use your height as a guide to determine the board size that best suits you. If you're under 4 feet (1.2 m) tall, consider buying a kid's deck, which is smaller than the usual 7 inches (17.75 cm). However, regardless of your height, the size you find most comfortable will likely be your best option.

WHEELS

They're exactly what they say they are. A skateboard rolls on four polyurethane wheels. They vary in size (always measured in millimeters) from 48 mm to 55 mm (1⅞ to 2⅛ inches) for the common skateboard, but most people prefer wheels that are

50 to 52 mm (1$^{15}\!/_{16}$ to 2$^{1}\!/_{16}$ inches). Wheels are also the most quickly worn out part of a skateboard setup. The hole in the center is where the truck axle fits through, and a divot inside is where the bearings are fitted.

The hardness of skateboard wheels is measured with a durometer and is indicated by the "A" rating. Hard wheels have an A rating around 100A, and they're best for speed on smooth surfaces, like what you find at skate parks. Hard wheels will give you a rough ride on concrete. Softer wheels, with an A rating of 90A or lower, provide a more comfortable ride on bumpy surfaces, but they're also slower.

TRUCKS

These are the axles that tie your board to your wheels and bearings. They allow your board to turn while you roll. They vary in size and height to match boards of different lengths and widths. Trucks come in three heights, low, mid and high. Low and mid trucks work best for street skating and flip tricks. High trucks allow you to ride on bigger wheels, so they're best for vert and ramp skating.

Trucks are made of aluminum and have two main parts, the baseplate and the hanger. The baseplate has holes and is the part that attaches to your board. The hanger hangs from the baseplate. A large bolt, called the kingpin, attaches the baseplate to the hanger. You can restrict or loosen your mobility by tightening or loosening the kingpin.

BEARINGS

It's the bearings that make your skateboard move, not the wheels themselves. Bearings are small metal circles that fit inside your wheels. In the middle they are filled with smaller metal ball bearings that spin. The truck axle fits through the hole in the center of the bearing and rests in the middle. Never oil your bearings or get them wet. Both will kill them pretty quickly.

HARDWARE

These are the nuts and bolts that bind your deck to your trucks. Nothing special here, just nuts and bolts.

GRIP TAPE

This is the sandpaper-type sticker on top of your deck. It's coarse surface creates friction with the rubber soles of your shoes, allowing you to control the board more easily.

How to BUY a Skateboard

You'd think buying a skateboard would be a fairly simple, straightforward process. And it is, for the most part, but there are some crucial things you should be aware of when purchasing a skateboard — first, there are huge differences in quality between boards depending on the retailer you buy from. A core shop, or a mall skateboard store like Zumiez, is going to have better quality goods. They'll last longer, work better and generally keep you (and whoever is buying your equipment for you) happy longer. Sporting goods stores sometimes have good products too, but it's best to avoid purchasing from department stores — I've yet to see a skateboard from a big box store that's not a total piece of junk.

A "complete" skateboard is one that comes with all of the parts and is pre-assembled. Generally they aren't of the best quality, but then they aren't the most expensive either. You're sacrificing the quality of the wheels, bearings, trucks and the board itself, but you're usually paying a third of the cost of buying all of the components separately. The size should be comfortable for you (meaning it shouldn't be higher than your shoulders when you're standing up with your board next to you). Most pre-made boards come in a fairly standard size, but nowadays companies realize that most of the people buying completes are parents of young children, so they have them in a slightly smaller size in addition to the regular size. The general rule is if you're under 4 feet (1.2 m) tall you should get the smaller child's sized board.

If you're just trying skateboarding out, then buying a complete is probably your best bet. If you get really into it, you can then purchase quality parts individually at a core skateboard store. This leads us to the other option when buying a skateboard: buying the parts individually and putting them together. This gives you plenty of choices of board sizes, shapes and graphics as well as wheel sizes and colors, truck colors, etc.

You should visit a store with your mom or dad and ask one of the salespeople to give you a rundown of what they have available, but, trust me, you're going to have very specific ideas of what you want your setup to be when you get *really* into skateboarding.

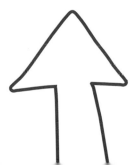

Putting Your Board Together

It's important to learn how to put your board together. Like any toy, sometimes parts break or become faulty and need to be replaced. Learning how to put a board together also means you can take it apart and repair it.

Tools You'll Need*

1. **screwdriver**

2. **knife**

3. **file**

4. **allen wrench**
(or allen key)

5. **skatetool**
(conventional wrench will also work)

* These tools should only be used under adult supervision and with the help of an adult.

Grip Your Deck

1 Remove the wax paper from the bottom of the grip tape.

2 Place the sticky side down on the nose and tail of your deck with even amounts of surplus on each side.

3 Flatten out your hand and slowly push the grip tape down on the board evenly. Make sure there are no air bubbles trapped underneath.

4 Once the grip is on the board, get an adult to help you with this next part. Get a file and rub it on the edges of your board. This creates an outline that you'll use to cut off the extra grip tape.

5 Get the adult to cut along the edge of your board with a knife, so that the grip tape is just covering the top of it, not the sides.

6 Use a bit of excess grip tape as sandpaper and smooth the edges of the gripped deck.

7 Flip your deck over and use an allen wrench (allen key) to punch holes through the grip tape where your hardware will go.

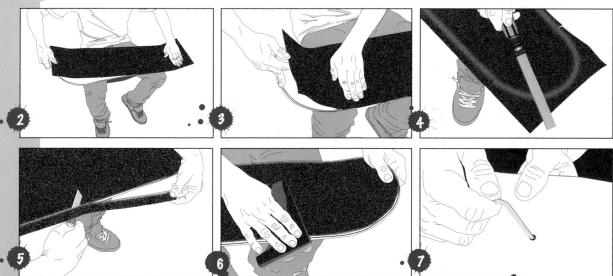

15

Attach the Trucks to the Deck

1 Starting at either the nose or tail of your deck, put your four bolts through the four holes you poked through the grip tape. It doesn't matter which end you start with.

2 Use one hand to keep the bolts pushed in and then flip your deck upside down. Put one set of trucks on, with the kingpin facing inward. The bolts should pop through the holes in the truck.

3 While still holding the bolts down, put the nuts onto the bolts as tight as you can with your fingers.

4 Once all four bolts are on, use an Allen wrench (Allen key) or screwdriver to tighten them as much as you can. The truck shouldn't be able to move at all if you've done it right. Repeat steps 1 to 4 with the other truck.

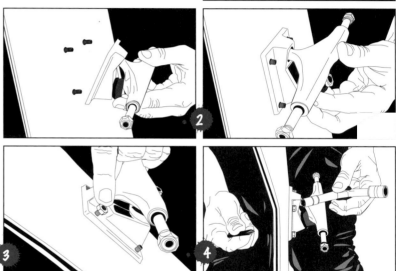

Fit the Bearings into the Wheels

1 Look at your wheels and note the indentation around the hole in the center. This is where your bearings fit into your wheels. The bearings can be a little tough to insert, but don't get discouraged.

2 Take the nut and washers off the end of one of your axles. Put them somewhere safe so you don't lose 'em. Put a

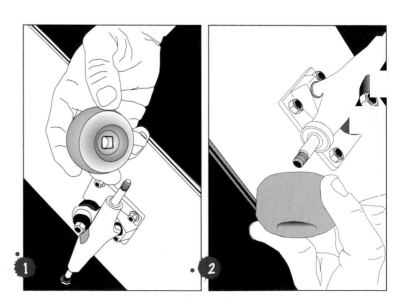

bearing on the axle and then grab a wheel and put it on the axle too, on top of the bearing.

3 With the board on the ground, push down on the wheel until you feel the bearing go into the wheel as far as possible.

4 Presto! You've inserted a bearing. Repeat for all your other wheels, until you've inserted bearings into both sides of all four wheels.

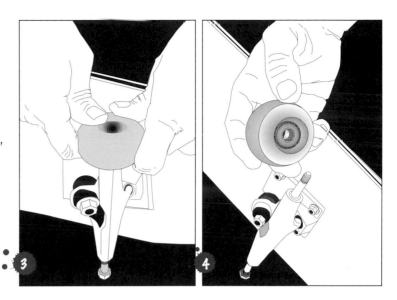

Attach the Wheels and Bearings to the Trucks

1 Take the bolt and one of the two washers off the end of the axle and put them in a safe place. Leave one washer on the axle. Place the wheel onto the axle so that the washer is between the wheel and the truck. Then, put the remaining washer on the axle so there are washers on both sides of your wheel.

2 Put the bolt on the axle against the wheel.

3 Tighten the bolt until the wheel doesn't move from side to side. Repeat for the other three wheels.

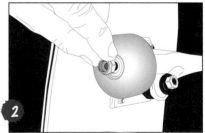

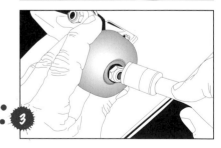

Tinker and Adjust

Now that your board is together, step on it and push yourself around a bit. If you feel like anything is loose, tighten it up with a skate tool. If your trucks are too tight or too loose when you're turning, adjust them. Now you're ready to go skate!

Safety Equipment

HELMETS

A helmet is a definite must for anyone learning to skateboard. You can get thrown off your board in an instant, so having proper head protection is just good sense. They come in every imaginable size, shape and color — frankly, helmets look just about as good as they're ever going to look. Just make sure you buy one approved by the U.S. Consumer Product Safety Commission or the Canadian Standards Association, otherwise the helmet may not be up to safety standards. Make sure you strap your helmet on properly, as per its instructions.

KNEE AND ELBOW PADS

Another must for anyone who is learning to skateboard are knee and elbow pads. They should fit snugly, but not so snugly that they restrict your mobility or blood flow. There are plenty of pads for biking that will work just fine for skateboarding, so don't feel like skateboard-specific pads are a requirement for safety.

WRIST GUARDS

Not a "must," but younger children skateboarding for the first time may want to consider using wrist guards. They're essentially gloves with a reinforced plastic or metal bar along the palm and wrist that protect against wrist injuries.

SHOES

Shoes aren't necessarily safety equipment, but, as with everything else, there are specific shoes that skateboarders tend to wear. Typically, skate shoes have extra padding around the ankle and in the tongue of the shoe, and good ones are often double stitched where wear and tear is most likely to occur: areas like where the sole meets the shoe along the toe. Skate shoes also have flat treads on along the bottom. You can skate in almost any shoe, but those that have nubs and bumps on the bottom of the sole (like cross trainers) will make it harder for you to control and feel your board underneath you.

Obstacles

BARRIER
They can be made of plastic or concrete; either way, you can slide, grind and stall on them.

BENCH
It's exactly the same a bench you sit on, but you slide or grind them instead.

BOWL
It's a cross between a shallow, round pool and a 360-degree mini-ramp. It's much like a pool but is easier to skate.

FLAT BAR
It's a long, square rail that's about 1 foot (30 cm) off the ground. They're usually found at skate parks.

FULL PIPE
It's a completely round pipe with no gaps in the surface except at the ends.

GAP
It's the empty space between two objects you skate over.

HALF PIPE a.k.a. VERT RAMP
Essentially just a large mini ramp, they vary from 10 to 16 feet (3 to 5 m) high. They have a lot more transition between the flat ground at the bottom and the coping at the top.

HIP
It's the side of a pyramid where two inclined planes meet without a flat part in between them. They can be at a 45- or 90-degree angle.

Concrete skate park featuring a full pipe, coping and quarter pipe transition.

Aerial image of a concrete skate park featuring bowls, quarter pipes, stair sets, hubbas, rails, pyramids, manny pads, ledges, benches, barriers and more.

HUBBA

It's a fat ledge down the side of a set of stairs.

LAUNCH RAMP

Also called a "kicker," it's a small ramp you skate up to give yourself a bit of air so you can do flip or grab tricks off of it.

LEDGE

Normally made of concrete, granite or marble, you grind or do slide tricks on ledges.

MANNY PAD

It's a large surface you ollie onto, perform a manual on and then hop off of. They come in all shapes and sizes.

MINI RAMP

They come in all shapes and sizes, but they're all the same — a flat bottom in the middle and transitions to coping on the sides.

PYRAMID

The pyramids at skate parks are just like the ones in Egypt, but they have a much less steep angle and a flat top. They're used to get air to do flip or grab tricks.

QUARTER PIPE

It's a transition that leads from flat ground to a coping.

RAIL

These are the hand rails on staircases that you grind or slide on. They vary in length.

STAIR SET

Just what it sounds like: it's a set of stairs you jump down while doing a trick. If there are two sets of stairs with a flat area separating them, it's called a double set.

WALL

It's exactly what it sounds like. You can skate a wall; it's called a wall ride.

Manny pads sit in the foreground of this skate park that also features vert ramps, a quarter pipe, rails, flat bars, hubbas and more.

Flat Ground Basics

Stance

One of the most important steps in learning to skateboard is figuring out your stance, or which foot is going to be in front of you when you ride your board.

Some people prefer to lead with their left foot (which we call "regular foot"), and some people would rather lead with their right foot (which we call "goofy foot," but it's not a diss). It's like being left-handed or right-handed — one's no better than the other, it's just personal preference.

The easiest way to figure out which stance you prefer is to try to slide across a slippery floor in your socks. The foot you instinctively throw out in front of you is likely the way you'd want to ride a skateboard too.

Left foot first? Congratulations, you're regular. Right foot first? Welcome to team goofy.

Now just so you're aware, when you lead with the opposite foot you'd naturally prefer to use, that's called riding "switch." It's WAAAAY more difficult, thus when someone says "Oh, he did that SWITCH!" it's like saying a right-handed baseball pitcher decided to throw with his left hand instead of his right.

Pushing

Now that you can stand on your board, it's time to start rolling. The way to make it happen is by pushing with your foot. It's a very easy process. Just whatever you do, don't push "mongo" (which is when you push with your front foot over the back bolts). Trust me, it's terrible and other kids *will* make fun of you. I will too.

Highlights:

1 Put your front foot on your board, over top of your front bolts but no further.

3 Bend your front leg and use your back foot to push yourself forward. Keep your weight focused on that front leg. You're not going to move very far yet, but it's a start.

5 Now that you're rolling, you need to repeat steps 3 and 4 again. Remember, keep your weight focused on your front foot. Repeat as needed until you've got the speed you want. When you're not pushing, keep your pushing foot (your back foot) between the back bolts and the tail of your board with your toes pointing outward.

29

Stopping

There are three methods to stopping on a skateboard, one for pretty much every occasion: when you can gingerly and leisurely take your time stopping, when you need to stop RIGHT NOW and somewhere in between.

Tail Skid

FOOT DRAG: The Slow and Easy Way to Stop

1 You're riding along, you see someone a few yards or meters ahead of you, and you want to roll over there and stop for a chat.

2 Keep your weight on your front foot and on your board while you gently hover your back foot above the ground beside your rear wheels (but make sure you don't touch the wheels!).

3 Lower your back foot until you feel the ground rub against the sole of your shoe — but don't just stomp your foot down! If you do that you're going to fall in a bad way. Just let your foot skim the ground.

4 Add pressure gradually as you slow down.

5 When you're at a near stop, shift your weight to your pushing/rear leg and stomp down to come to a complete stop.

TAIL SKID: The "You've Got a Little Bit of Time to Stop" Stop

1 Place your back foot on the tail of your board and hang your heel off the edge.

2 Throw all of your weight on your back foot and force the tail of your board and the heel of your back foot on the ground.

3 Lean back into it to keep yourself balanced until you come to a complete stop.

POWERSLIDE: When You Need to Stop Right Now!

1 You're riding along and you suddenly need to stop immediately.

2 With both feet facing outward in the same direction, carve your board until you've turned so your toes are pointed in front of you.

3 Dig in your heels quickly so your board stays sideways and you're facing forward.

4 Lean back, dig in those heels and let the friction of the wheels stop you. Make sure you're aware of your balance and adjust your weight once you've slowed down, or you're going to fall on your butt.

Kicking Your Board Up

This is a simple thing that you'll do every day, but it's not something normally taught to kids — you're just expected to figure it out on your own. Forget that! I'm just going to tell you how to do it so we can all save some time, okay? Being able to get your board from the ground to your hand quickly is a skill you're definitely going to want to have, otherwise you'll be stuck bending over a billion times a day to grab your board.

Highlights:

3 Put one of your feet on the tail of your board.

4 Push down sharply, slapping the tail against the ground. This will pop the nose of your board up toward you. Move your foot out of the way after you slap it down so your toes don't stop the board from coming all the way up to you.

5 Keep your hand out, ready to catch the nose of your board.

6 Catch the nose and walk away.

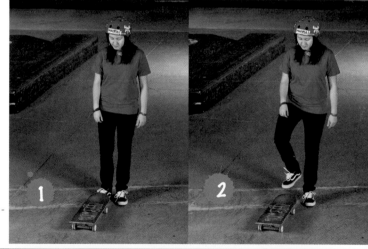

Turning

Riding in a straight line is pretty boring, and not knowing how to turn could lead you to longboarding. No one wants that.

There's two basic ways to turn your board: carving is how you turn when you are rolling with speed; kick turns are for when you are slowly rolling around.

CARVING *(pictured below)*
Highlights:

1 Roll along with one foot forward or both pointing out toward the same side.

2 Shift your weight forward or backward on your feet (toward the direction you want to turn in), and lean your body in that direction as well. That shift in weight on your trucks and wheels will turn the board in your desired direction.

KICK TURN *(not shown)*

1 Put your back foot between the bolts and tail of your board. Lean in the direction you wish to go, raising your front foot slightly while maintaining a normal amount of weight on your back foot. This will send the nose of your board upward.

2 The nose is easier to move when it's up in the air, so kick or pull it in the direction you want to go, using the grip tape to hold your board with your foot.

3 When your board is facing the direction you want to go, put your weight back down on your front foot. Repeat steps 1 through 3 as needed.

How to Fall

The sad reality is that you're going to fall off your board. A lot. And you will sometimes get hurt too. That's what skateboarding is, frankly. It's a lot of falling down and getting back up. But it builds character, or so I'm told…

Something as simple as rolling on a rock or a crack in the sidewalk can send you flying forward — the best thing you can do is learn how to fall.

What's most important is that when you fall, accept that you are no longer on your board and you aren't going to be able to save this. Throwing your arms out to catch yourself is only going to make it hurt worse. Instead, accept your fate and try to do the following.

Highlights:

3 Tuck your chin into your chest and keep your arms tight to your body.

4 Roll into the ground with your shoulder, letting it hit the ground first (if you can). Not an ideal solution, but it's better than breaking your wrist or elbow, right?

5 Go limp. If you managed to land shoulder first, you'll roll with the momentum you've gained. If you land on your bum, you'll roll onto your back. Either way, being stiff is only going to make it hurt more.

33

Nollie

The nollie is essentially the mirror opposite of the ollie. You're popping the board off the ground, but instead of using your back foot and the tail of the board, you'll be using your front foot and the nose. It's a little awkward at first, but you'll get the hang of it.

Highlights:

1 Squat down on your board with your front foot on the nose and your back foot just in front of the back bolts.

4 This next movement is the same as the ollie, but backward. Kick down on your board with your front foot, which will send the tail up toward you. Don't let your front foot touch the ground for long; keep in mind that it's a quick motion, just like this step for the ollie.

5 When the tail jumps up toward you, drag your back foot toward the tail along the grip tape, lifting your foot (and the board) up with you. Keep that front foot tucked up as the board levels out.

6 Your board is now heading up in the air, and you're above it with your feet hovering over the trucks. Or at least, that's what should be happening. Keep the board lined up with your body using your feet, and try to make your board as level as possible, keeping your feet over the bolts.

7 Bend your knees with your feet centered on the board and land. Roll away happy.

Manual

A manual is hard to do and takes a lot of practice to get on lock. It's all about balance. It's kind of like playing on a teeter-totter that's on wheels and constantly trying to throw you off. Finding the sweet spot of balance isn't easy, but once you get it, it's totally worthwhile because manuals look really cool. Practice makes perfect, so get ready to fail a lot before you succeed.

Highlights:

1 Speed is key to maintaining a manual, so build up decent speed before you try a manny.

4 Ollie up and above the obstacle. Keep your shoulders square with the obstacle.

5 Put your back foot on the tail of your board and your front foot over the front bolts. Next, as you land your ollie, lean back on the tail and balance on that back truck.

6 Keep a little extra weight on your back foot to keep the nose up, but not so much weight that it sends the tail to the ground. Your back leg should be fairly straight at this point. Your front leg should be bent, so it can act as a counterbalance.

7 Don't forget to use your arms to help keep you balanced. If you start to dip forward, drop your back arm to pull the nose of your board back up. When you find the sweet spot, hold on for as long as you can. If you start to lose it, shift your weight forward, as you'll be less likely to bail that way.

9 When you reach the end of the obstacle, level out your board with your front foot while you let your back wheels roll off the edge.

11 Land with all four wheels hitting the ground at the same time.

Slides

Board Slide

This is the easiest slide you're going to learn, period. This trick has a lot of forgiveness when you're sliding, as the trucks on either side are generally keeping you in place — plus, more often than not you're usually able to bail out of it super easily by hopping off your board.

You may not think so when you're learning it, but someday this is going to be your "sleep through it" warm-up trick. Trust me.

Highlights:

1 Line yourself up with your obstacle and build up a decent amount of speed as you roll toward it. You should enter the trick with your toes pointing away from the obstacle.

4 Ollie up and above the obstacle. Keep your shoulders square with the obstacle you're sliding.

5 When you're above the obstacle, put the front truck of your board over to the far side of the obstacle, putting the center of your board on the obstacle.

6 Keep those feet on the bolts (if you can) and evenly distribute your weight on both feet. Keep your knees bent and your shoulders facing the direction you're sliding in. Whatever you do, keep looking forward.

7 Use those arms to keep yourself balanced as you slide along.

8 Get ready to straighten yourself out when you see the end of the obstacle coming.

9 As you pop off the end of the obstacle, twist yourself so that you *and* your board are straightened out.

10 Land with both sets of wheels hitting the ground at the same time if you can. Roll away.

Lip Slide

You're going to be shocked to learn that this trick is very similar to the last trick you learned. Crazy right? Well, as you'll soon see, the lipslide is essentially a boardslide, except with the lipslide you enter to trick from the opposite side, and when you ollie onto the obstacle you are looking away from the direction you're sliding in. That can, frankly, make it a little scary. But if you play your cards right, this can be a really fun trick to pull out at the skate park.

Highlights:

1 Line yourself up with your obstacle and build up a decent amount of speed as you roll toward it. You should enter the trick with your toes pointing toward the obstacle.

5 Ollie up and above the obstacle. Make sure you've got good pop on this one — you need that height!

7 When you're midair, turn your whole body so that your back foot rotates from behind you to the far side of the obstacle. When you land, the tail of your board should be off the obstacle, on the opposite side from the side your rode in on. Put your feet on the bolts, evenly distribute your weight and keep both of your knees slightly bent and your board centered on the obstacle. Remember to use your arms to balance yourself.

8 This is the tricky part. As you see the end of the obstacle getting closer, get ready to straighten yourself back out but put your lead shoulder forward. Keep your head turned so you can see your landing spot and the end of the obstacle.

9 When you pop off the end of the obstacle, twist yourself around quickly so you and your board are both facing forward, nose first.

10 Aim to land all four wheels on the ground at the same time.

44

Tail Slide

Alright, by now you're comfortable sliding your board and not necessarily facing the direction you're sliding in. Let's crank it up a notch with the tailslide.

The trick here is to put *all* of your weight on the tail of your board. It's a little weird compared to what you've already learned — you'll likely feel like you should put less weight on your back foot and the tail of your board in an attempt to slide further, but that's just wrong, dude. You want to slide further? Roll into the trick with more speed.

Highlights:

1 Line yourself up with your obstacle and build up a decent amount of speed as you roll toward it. Enter the trick with your toes pointing toward to obstacle.

3 Ollie up and above the obstacle.

4 When you're in the air, turn your body 90 degrees, so the tail of your board is over the obstacle. At the same time, push your board to the side and onto the obstacle.

5 Put most of your weight on your back foot, on the tail of your board, and find the balance between not enough weight and so much weight that you're stalling out. The tail should be flat against the obstacle, and the board should be straight across the edge. Keep your front foot resting lightly over the other set of bolts.

6 Keep your knees bent and use your arms to balance yourself.

7 Get ready to straighten yourself out for the end of the grind.

8 As you pop off the edge of the obstacle, turn your lead shoulder and hips forward to help kick the nose of your board out in front of you. That'll make you land straight.

9 Try to land on all four wheels at the same time and roll away.

Grinds

50-50 Grind

This is the go-to grind. It's fairly easy to do and easy to learn. It's essentially an axle stall (see pages 86–87), but instead of standing still you're "grinding" along on your trucks.

The key is to combine speed and balance. You have to move fast enough so you can grind the entire length of the obstacle you're on while also keeping your weight distributed evenly on both feet so you don't fall off the obstacle.

Highlights:

1 Build up a decent amount of speed and line yourself up with your obstacle as you roll toward it.

3 Ollie up and above the obstacle. Keep your shoulders lined up with the obstacle you're grinding.

4 Once you're on top of the obstacle, push your board down with both feet. Lock those trucks onto the obstacle. If you can, try to get the trucks down at the same time.

6 Use your arms to keep yourself balanced, moving them as needed to keep yourself upright.

8 As you reach the end of your grind, lift your front truck up a little bit and let yourself sail off the obstacle.

10 Try to put all four wheels down at the same time as you land.

12 Roll away.

53

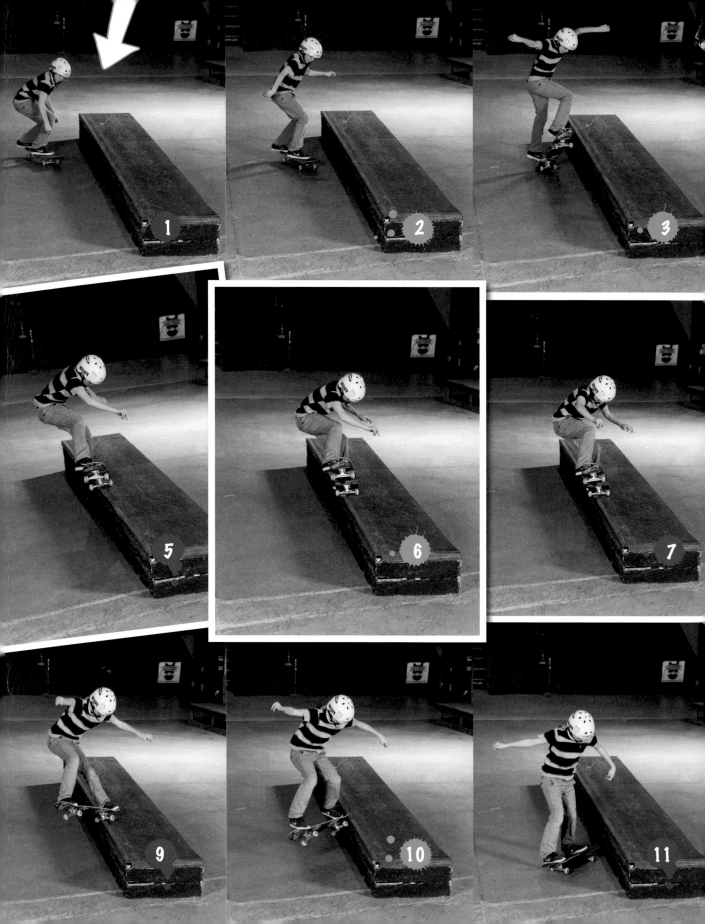

5-0 Grind

Similar to a 50-50 grind, a 5-0 grind (pronounced "five oh") is essentially half of a 50 50 grind: you're only grinding the back truck, while the front truck is up and off the obstacle. It's kind of like a manual, but instead of balancing your wheels on the ground you're balancing your back truck on an obstacle.

Highlights:

1 Get your obstacle lined up with your body and build up some decent speed as you approach.

4 Ollie up and above the obstacle you want to grind.

5 When you're above the obstacle, push your back foot down and lock that back truck on top of the obstacle. Keep the nose of your board up — you can rest your front foot on it, but don't push down.

7 As you grind, look ahead to where you intend to land. Get ready.

9 When you reach the end of your grind, pop off the obstacle and then push your front foot down on the front truck and level out your board so you can land evenly.

11 As you fall to the ground, try to put all four wheels down at the same time.

12 Roll away.

Nose Grind

I hate to break it to you, but a nose grind isn't terribly original — it's just a 5-0 grind, but instead of grinding on the back truck you're grinding your front truck. I'm sorry if this disappoints you.

The good news is, if you've got 5-0 grinds on lock, then you should have no problem adding a nose grind to your bag of tricks. It's just a little bit harder because all of your weight and balance is in front of you.

Highlights:

1 Build up a good amount of speed, enough to carry you through the grind, and then line yourself up to the obstacle.

4 Ollie up and above the obstacle you plan to grind.

5 When you're above the obstacle, push your front foot down and lock your front truck onto the obstacle. Make sure your foot is between the nose of the board and the front bolts. Your back foot should be over your back bolts. Don't cheat and let your nose drag on the obstacle either.

7 Use those arms to keep yourself balanced. Keep an eye out for the end of the grind, and get ready for your landing.

9 Grind right off the end of the obstacle, but at the end give a slight nollie (see pages 36–37) to pop yourself completely off the obstacle.

10 Push your back foot down onto the back truck and level out your board so you can land evenly, with all four wheels hitting the ground at the same time.

11 Roll away.

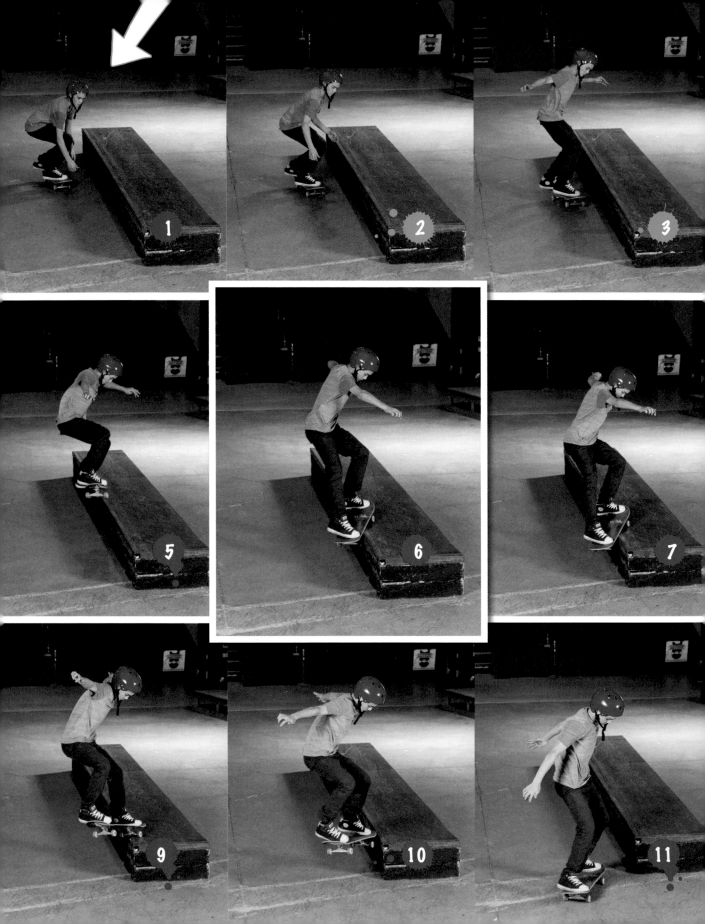

Smith Grind

I've got good news and bad news. The good news is that once you've got smith grinds down it's going to be a go-to trick, because once you're locked into one, there's not much you can do to get knocked out of it outside of leaning forward too much. The bad news? It's a hard trick to learn.

The way it works is you grind on the back truck while you keep your front truck hanging off the side of the obstacle and keep the toe-side edge of your board sliding on its edge.

Confusing? Let's break it down.

Highlights:

1 Line yourself up with the obstacle so that you're facing it.

4 Ollie up and above the obstacle you intend to grind.

5 When you're above the obstacle, line up your back truck to land directly on the obstacle while positioning the nose of your board to fall off the same edge of the obstacle from where you entered the trick. Keep both feet on the bolts.

6 Now that you've landed on the obstacle, grind your back truck and slide on the toe edge of your board. Make sure your entire weight is on your back foot and your back knee is bent. Your front leg should be straight, and the toes of your front foot should be pointing out and down, locking your board onto the obstacle.

7 Use your arms to keep yourself balanced. Stay lined up with the obstacle.

9 When you see the end of the obstacle coming, put a little pressure on your back foot to lift the nose up off the obstacle and then grind straight off of it.

10 Let your back truck clear the obstacle on the way off, and then straighten out your board as you head to the ground.

11 Aim, as always, to have all four wheels hit the ground at the same time — or as close as you can get to the same time.

Feeble Grind

It's the best-looking grind in skateboarding — the feeble grind. It's similar to the smith grind, except that instead of the board hanging off the side you rode in from, it hangs off the opposite side. Honestly, there's not much else to say about it other than it's awesome and you're going to be stoked you learned how to do 'em. Let's get to it.

Highlights:

1 Line yourself up with the obstacle you're going to grind, and get enough speed so that you can make it through the whole grind without getting hung up.

4 Ollie up and above the obstacle you intend to grind.

5 When you're above the obstacle, line the middle of your board up with the obstacle.

6 Land on your back truck. As soon as your back truck hits the obstacle, lean back and extend your front foot so the bottom of your board rests on the obstacle. Both the back truck and the center of your board should be on the obstacle, and your front truck should be hanging off the side. Do not let that front truck touch the obstacle, or you'll be in trouble.

7 As always, you must try to keep your feet over the bolts. Rest most of your weight on your back foot, with only a little weight on your front foot. Use your arms to balance yourself, and keep your shoulders parallel to the obstacle you're grinding.

9 Keep an eye out for the end of the obstacle and get ready to land. The dismount may feel a little strange.

10 When you clear the obstacle and are heading toward the ground, straighten the board out and try to land all four wheels on the ground at the same time.

11 Roll away stoked.

Crooked Grind

If you've got nose grinds on lock, you're not far away from having a crooked grind in your... uh... trick portfolio?

The two tricks are very similar. When you're doing a nose grind (see pages 56–57), the tail of your board is parallel with the obstacle, but with a crooked grind, the tail juts out to the side at an angle — it's crooked. That angle makes balancing a lot harder, but thankfully you can let your nose drag on the obstacle with a crooked grind — it's socially acceptable.

All that said, these tricks aren't very different from each other. Let's see if you can make it happen first try.

Highlights:

1 Line yourself up with your obstacle and build up a decent amount of speed as you roll toward it.

4 Ollie above the obstacle. Keep your shoulders lined up with the obstacle you're going to grind.

5 Now that you're up and on the obstacle, line up the nose and front truck of your board with the obstacle. Keep the tail hanging off the side at a sharp angle, and have your front foot between the bolts and the nose of your board.

6 Lock your front truck onto the obstacle by pushing your front foot down and drag the nose on the obstacle too. Most of your weight should be on your front foot, with your back foot hovering above the rear bolts.

7 Make sure the tail is hanging off to the side at an angle. Use your arms to balance yourself on the front truck, and try to keep your shoulders squared up with the obstacle.

8 Let yourself grind right off the end of the obstacle.

9 When you clear the end, start straightening out your board while also leveling it out by bringing the tail down.

10 Try to land with all four wheels hitting the ground at the same time. Roll away.

Flip Tricks

Kick Flip

A kick flip is done by spinning the board sideways, top over bottom, just once. The nose and tail always stay facing the same direction they were in at the beginning of the trick.

Height is the most important thing for a kick flip. The higher you can pop your ollie (see pages 34–35), the more time your board has to rotate without catching the ground before it's done. If you do it right, it will look awesome. If you do it wrong, you will *not* look very awesome. So take your time, and think it through.

Highlights:

1 Get rolling at a decent speed that you're comfortable with.

4 Ollie up, popping off the ground as high as possible. The higher you get, the more time the board has to spin, so pop that ollie!

5 Just as you do for an ollie, drag your front foot forward to bring your board up. But as you drag your front foot up, kick the board toward you with your toe, making it flip.

6 Keep your feet tucked up underneath you so the board has room to spin. Watch the board below you. Once it spins a full flip and you see grip tape again, get your feet in position to catch the board. Aim to have both feet landing on the bolts.

7 Catch the board with your back foot first, then with your front foot. Keep your knees bent and ready for landing. Try to even the board out so you land on all four wheels at the same time (or as close as possible).

9 Stomp that landing and roll away.

67

Heel Flip

A heel flip is essentially the same as a kick flip (see pages 66–67). The only difference is instead of kicking the board toward you with your toe, you kick it away from you with your heel. (Which is why it's called a heel flip. Duh.)

But thankfully, everything you learned for the kick flip will come into play here. A lot of skaters will tell you heel flips are easier to learn than kick flips. If you're one of those people, and you've spent a month on the previous pages trying to learn kick flips — sorry dude! Should have told you to start here.

Highlights:

1 Get a comfortable amount of speed and then get ready to ollie off the ground. But instead of centering your front foot on your board, let the toes of your front hang off your board slightly. Put the ball of your back foot on the heel edge of the tail.

4 Ollie up. As with the kick flip, height is your friend here. Get that board up as high as possible.

5 As you drag the toes of your front foot forward during the ollie, kick your board away from you using the heel of your front foot. This will make the board flip underneath you. Keep your eyes on the board underneath you. You'll see the bottom of the board as it flips.

6 After the board spins all the way around and you see grip tape under you again, catch the board with your back foot. Aim for those bolts!

7 Keep your knees bent, get both feet on top of the bolts and get ready to land.

9 Stomp it and roll away happy.

Pop Shove-it

Well, time to take it up a notch in difficulty. The pop shove-it (sometimes spelled shuv) spins your board nose to tail by 180 degrees, so that when you land the nose is behind you and the tail is in front of you. Your wheels stay facing the ground and your grip tape stays facing up — you'll be spinning your board almost the way a basketball player spins a ball on his fingertip.

It's going to take a lot more coordination than a kick or heel flip, which makes it a little harder to learn at first, but once you get the hang of it you'll find this is a go-to trick.

Highlights:

1   Get a comfortable amount of speed.

6   Time to "pop." Keep your back foot closer to the toe-side edge of the board than you normally would for an ollie, and let the big toe of your back foot hang over the side a little bit. Instead of popping the board up, like for an ollie, you'll be "scooping" it by slapping it down with your back foot and catching it with those hanging toes.

7   As you scoop up the board, flick the tail of the board behind you with your hanging toes. This will begin to turn the board. Help it along by gently kicking the nose of the board forward, away from you, with your front foot. This is the "shove" part of the trick.

8   Keep those feet up and your eyes on the board as it spins below you.

9   When the board has turned 180 degrees (so the nose is behind you and the tail is in front of you), catch it with your front foot and bring it back beneath you. Aim for the bolts with both feet. Keep your knees bent and get ready to land.

10   Stomp that landing, and, hey, you're rolling away fakie!

Varial Flip

Time to combine what you've learned so far. We're going to mash together the pop shove-it (see pages 70–71) and kick flip (see pages 66–67) and make a whole new trick — the varial flip. To do it, you'll be turning the board from nose to tail and from top to bottom, all in one move. It's definitely going to be a step up from what we've done before, but if you're not making your skating better, what's the point of skating at all?

Highlights:

1 Get a comfortable amount of speed.

5 Stomp your back foot down to pop the board up, but as you do, scoop it out behind you with the toes of your back foot, like a pop shove-it. This will send the tail of the board behind you.

6 Next, just like you would with an ollie, drag your front foot up along the board and then kick your front foot out like for a kick flip.

7 Keep your feet up and your eyes down as the board spins both ways. Get your feet ready to catch the board.

8 When you see the tail underneath your front foot, catch the board with your front foot first, then with your back foot.

9 Keep your knees bent and your feet on the bolts.

11 Land it and roll away.

73

360 Flip

This is the hardest flip trick in this book. Sorry. If it makes you feel any better, even people who've been skating for years have a hard time with this one.

We'll be taking the varial flip (see pages 72–73) to another level. Instead of turning the board 180 degrees like a pop shove-it, we'll be letting it spin around a complete 360-degree turn, so you land on the board the same way you took off from it.

This trick is called a 360 flip, and it's going to make you VERY frustrated. Hang in there, you'll get it eventually. I hope.

Highlights:

1 Get a comfortable amount of speed.

3 Stomp your back foot down to pop the board up. As you do, scoop the board out with the toes of your back foot, like a pop shove-it, but scrape the tail in a quick half-circle motion with enough strength to spin the board a complete turn. This will send the tail of the board behind you.

4 This is the key moment. Once you scoop the tail, the nose will pop up a little bit. Kick the nose out with your front foot, just like you do when you're doing a varial flip. This will send the board flipping top over bottom as it spins nose to tail.

5 Keep those feet up and your eyes on the board.

6 Once you see the nose in front of you and the grip tape under you, catch the board with your front foot and guide it back underneath you. Get your back foot on the back bolts.

7 Bend your knees and make sure your feet are on top of the bolts.

9 Land it, and roll away a happy young man or woman.

Transition Basics

Pumping

Dropping into a pool or onto a ramp will give you enough speed to roll back and forth twice at best. If you want to keep skating and enjoying the transition, you'll need to learn to keep the party going. Pumping is the key.

Pumping gives you a little boost of speed between trips to the coping. It's like you're on a swing and you're kicking your legs to keep going higher. If you learn to pump properly, you can skate transition all day long.

Highlights:

4 When you roll up the transition, straighten your legs out from the knees-bent position you normally roll around in.

5 As you reach as high up the tranny as you can get and feel yourself about to come back down, squat down.

7 When you reach the sweet spot of the transition (just before it goes flat, as pictured), straighten your legs quickly. That switch from squatting to standing will help push you forward.

9 Repeat when you hit the other side of the transition as needed.

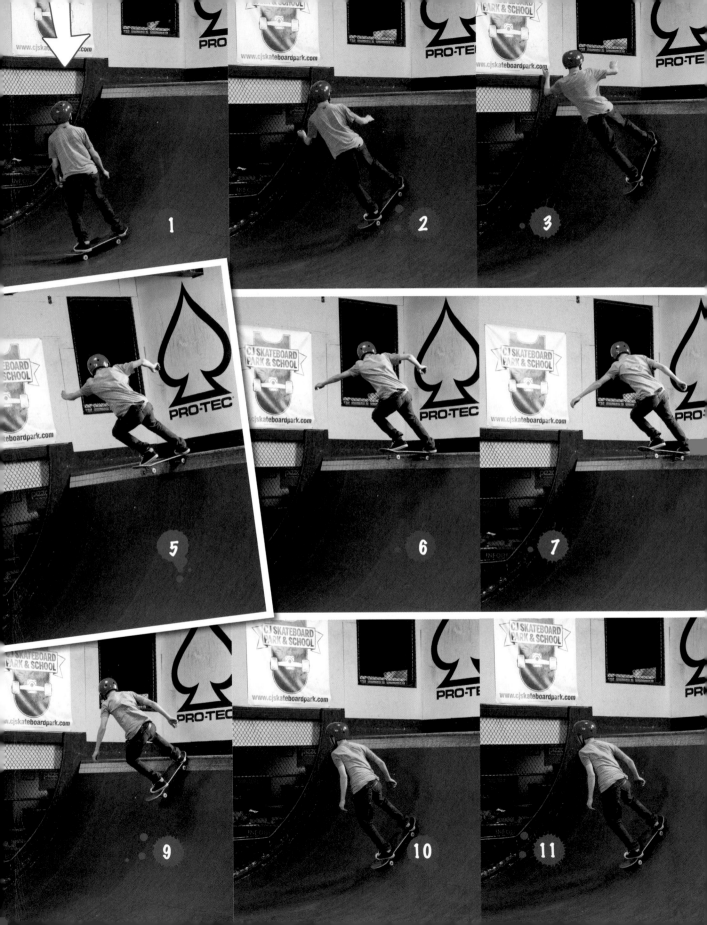

1

2

3

5

6

7

9

10

11

Stalls

Stalls are very aptly named — you are basically using them to stall for time to set up your tricks in between rolling from one coping of the transition to the other. There's not much to them, but they're very important.

There are two types of stalls: nose and tail. One uses the nose of your board, and one uses the tail. Nose and tail stalls are, for our purposes, the same thing but in reverse: you're pressing your nose or tail on the coping so you can stop for a quick second before rolling back to the other side of the transition.

Highlights:

1 Roll up to the coping with your front foot on the nose for a nose stall and the tail for a tail stall.

4 Just as your wheels are about to hit the coping, push your front foot down to press your tail or nose (depending on the direction you're going in) against the coping.

6 Put all of your weight on your forward foot so you can rest on the coping for a second or two.

8 Lean your weight back from the coping, onto your back foot (which will now become your front foot), and just like dropping in, let gravity pull you back down into the ramp.

Rock 'n Rolls

It's just another way to buy you time between tricks on transition, but why'd they name it rock 'n roll? Well it was invented by one Lemmy Kilmeister, who, in case you aren't aware, is the lead singer and bassist of the bad boys of rock 'n roll, Motorhead. That's actually a lie. There's not much to say about rock 'n rolls, but at least they're fun to do.

Highlights:

5 When you're in transition and headed up toward the coping, keep your knees bent and make sure you go high enough so that the middle of your board is over the coping.

6 Once your front wheels are past the coping and your board is halfway up, push down on the front on your board with your front foot so your front wheels touch the deck.

8 The wheels hitting the deck will make a "ca-chunk" sound. Once you hear that, put your weight on your back foot, which will lift the front of your board off the deck and over the coping.

9 When the front wheels are up, pivot off the rear truck and turn yourself around 180 degrees, so you're now facing the opposite direction. This will bring your front wheels around in front and will make you face the ramp nose first.

10 Now that you're facing down the ramp, put your front wheels down and roll away.

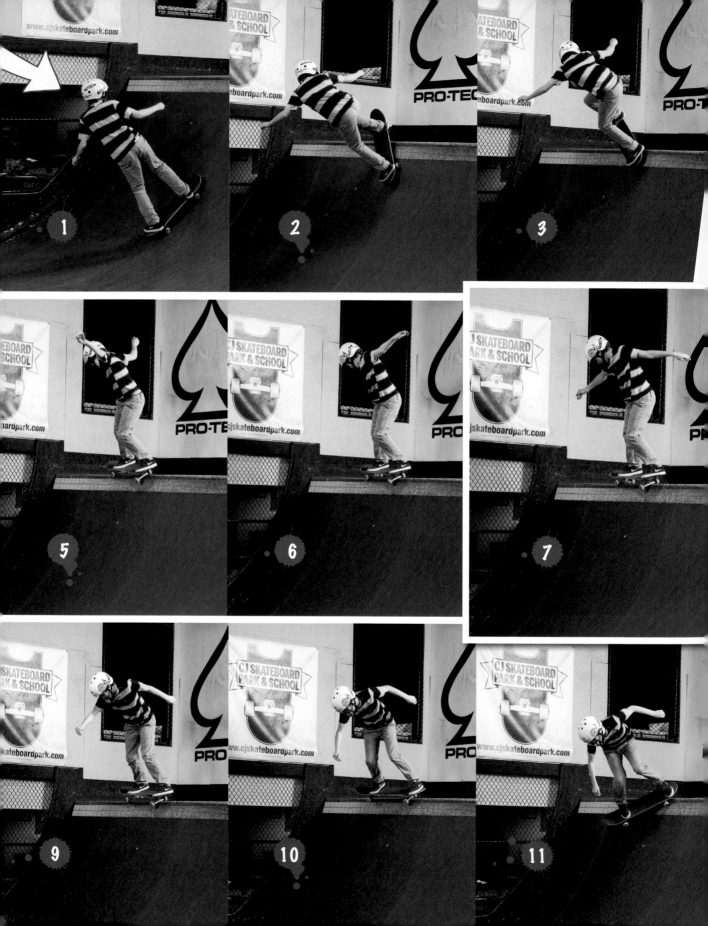

Axle Stalls

This is the same idea as the nose or tail stall — you're buying time between trips to each coping. This time around, you're going to rest your trucks on the coping just like in a 50-50 grind (see pages 52–53), but you won't be moving as much. Remember that if you ride toward the coping too fast and at an angle, you're going to grind it. Make sure you're riding straight toward the coping so your speed and momentum carry you upward and don't send you grinding along the coping.

Highlights:

2 Roll up to the coping and lift your front truck over the coping. Make sure you raise your truck enough to clear the coping.

3 Then let your back truck reach the coping, but do not let it go past it.

4 Turn your body and board so you're lined up with the coping. Keep most of your weight on your back foot, staying balanced.

7 Once you're lined up on the coping and steady, put your front truck down by shifting your weight so its spread out evenly on both legs, over the board.

8 Stay balanced on the coping until you're ready to roll back in.

10 When you're ready to roll back in, shift your weight to your back truck to lift the front of your board off the coping. Pivot on the back truck and move the front truck back toward the transition.

11 Shift your weight off your back foot and let your back truck come off the coping. Roll on in.

Glossary

360 flip
A trick that involves flipping the board a full 360 degrees underneath the rider.

Am
Short for amateur, ams are the level below pro skateboarders. They make a living from skateboarding but don't have signature products (and so don't collect royalties).

Axle
The metal rod on a truck, which runs the width of the skate deck and from which the wheels hang.

Back foot
Also known as the pushing foot, the back foot is normally placed behind the skater.

Backside
A trick in which the rider leads up to the obstacle with the heels facing it.

Banana board
Skateboards from the 1950s and 60s that were very narrow, around 6–7 inches (15–18 cm), and that did not have a bend in the nose or tail.

Bank to bank
A skate obstacle that runs from a surface that slopes up to a flat top and then to a surface that slopes down.

Barrier
There are a couple of different types of plastic and concrete barriers. Depending on the setup, skaters can grind, stall and slide on them.

Baseplate
The top of a truck. It's made of flat metal and has holes that allow the truck to be attached to the skate deck.

Bearing
A hollow, round metal casing filled with greased ball bearings. It attaches to a skateboard wheel and makes the wheel spin.

Bench
An obstacle that is the same as the benches we sit on. Skateboarders do grinds and slides on them.

360 flip

Bolt
Two sets of nuts and bolts that attach the trucks to the skate deck.

Bowl
A combination of a shallow, round pool and a 360-degree mini ramp.

Bushing
Small rubber circles that cushion the truck when it turns. They are located around the kingpin.

Carving
A way to change direction by shifting body weight while rolling quickly.

Coping
The lip at the top of a transition. On a ramp, it's the metal tube that joins the deck and the ramp. It is where skaters perform grinds and slides.

Deck
The top part of a ramp or a pool, which is where a skater stands before dropping in. Not to be confused with a skate deck.

Double set
Two sets of stairs with a bit of flat ground between. Skaters do tricks on them.

Dropping in
Entering a transition, such as a ramp.

Fakie
Riding backward while in a normal stance.

Filmer
Someone who films skateboarding with a video camera.

Dropping in

Flat bar
A long, square rail, usually found at a skate park, that's laid about a foot (30 cm) off the ground. Skaters do grinds and slides on them.

Flat bottom (or flat)
The flat part of the ramp, between the two transitions.

Flip trick
Any trick where the rider flips the board, either top over bottom or from nose to tail (or vice versa).

Flow rider
A skater who gets free stuff from skate companies but doesn't make a living from skateboarding.

Foot drag
Stopping by dragging a foot off the tail of the board.

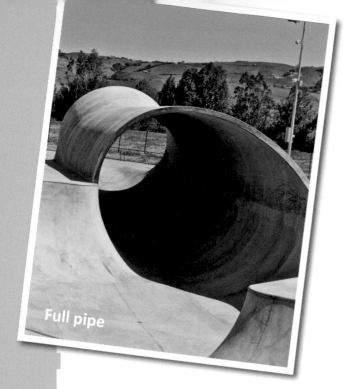
Full pipe

Front foot
The foot that stays on the skate deck while the skater pushes. The front foot is, obviously, the foot that stays in front of the skater.

Frontside
A trick in which the rider leads up to the obstacle with the toes facing it.

Full pipe
A completely rounded half pipe with no gaps in the surface other than the ends. Skaters just carve around in these.

Gap
The empty space between any two objects that a skateboarder jumps over. They can be the same height, or one can be higher than the other.

Goofy
A skateboard stance where the right foot is in front.

Grab
A trick that involves grabbing the board while skating transition. (Grabs are advanced tricks and are not covered in this book.)

Graphics
The artwork on the bottom of a skate deck.

Grind
Any trick that involves balancing on one or both trucks and sliding along an object. Riders can grind handrails, concrete or marble ledges, benches and many other obstacles.

Grip tape
Black sandpaper with glue on one side that is placed on the top of a skate deck. Grip tape creates friction between the board and the skater's shoes, allowing the skater to control the board.

Half pipe (or vert ramp)
10- to 16-foot (3 to 4.9 m) high mini ramps with an extended space between the transition and the coping.

Hanger
The part of the truck that hangs below the baseplate.

Heel flip
A trick that involves the rider kicking the board using the heel of the foot to make the board spin top over bottom.

Hip
The sides of a pyramid; two flat and sloped surfaces that meet without a flat part in between them. They can have a 45- to 90-degree angle.

Hubba

The fat ledge down the side of a set of stairs.

Kick flip

A trick that involves the rider kicking the board with the toes to make it spin top over bottom.

Kick turn

A way to turn by kicking the nose of the board in the desired direction.

Kingpin

The large bolt in the middle of a truck. It is tightened or loosened to control how easily a skater can turn.

Launch ramp (or kicker)

These were and remain a mainstay of suburban skating, as many suburbs still do not have skate parks or ramps. It's a small ramp skaters skate up to give themselves a bit of air so they can do flip or grab tricks.

Ledge

An obstacle normally made of concrete, granite or, ideally, marble. Skaters do grind or slide tricks on them.

Manny pad

A large, flat, rectangular surface that skaters perform manuals on.

Manual (or manny)

A trick that involves balancing on only one set of wheels. A regular manual is when the rider balances on the wheels at the tail of the board. A nose manual is when the rider balances on the wheels at the nose of the board.

Mini ramp

They vary in size, but all mini ramps have the same characteristics: a flat bottom in the middle and transitions to coping on either side. A skater can do just about any trick on a mini.

Mongo

When a rider pushes with the back foot over the front bolts.

Nollie

The mirror opposite of an ollie, this trick involves the skateboarder popping the board up using the back foot and nose of the board.

Nose

The end of the skate deck that is less curved inward. It is pointed in front of the skater.

Manual

Ollie
A trick that involves the skateboarder popping the board up using the back foot and tail of the board. It is the foundation of many other tricks.

Pole
A traffic sign or a barrier pole that is bent enough so a skateboarder can skate it.

Pool
A large obstacle that is similar to an empty inground swimming pool.

Pop shove-it
A trick that involves rotating the board 180 degrees nose to tail.

Powerslide
Stopping by digging in the heels and leaning back.

Pros
Skateboarders who make a living from skateboarding and collect royalties from signature boards, shoes, wheels, trucks and clothing.

Pumping
Skateboarders pump their legs up and down to give themselves momentum while skating transition.

Pyramid
Mostly seen at skate parks, this obstacle is the same shape as the ones in Egypt, just at a less steep angle and with a flat top. Skaters use them to get height to do flip or grab tricks in midair.

Quarter pipe
A transition that leads from flat ground to a coping. It looks like a mini ramp cut in four quarters.

Rail
Handrails on staircases that skateboarders do tricks on or over.

Regular stance
A skateboard stance where the left foot is in front.

Rock 'n Roll
A trick that involves a rider briefly balancing the deck of the board on the coping while skating transition.

Shop rider
A skateboarder who is sponsored by a skate shop.

Skateboard
The deck, trucks, wheels, bearings, bolts and grip tape completely assembled.

Skate deck
The wooden board a skateboarder stands on.

Skateboard

Stall

Skate tool

A multi-tool used to put together a skateboard. Designs vary but always include some sort of wrench.

Slide

Any trick that involves using the underside of the skate deck to slide along an obstacle.

Stair set

A set of stairs at a skate park. Skaters do tricks on them.

Stall

A trick that is designed to give riders a pause while skating transition so they can set up other, more complicated, tricks. There are three types of stalls: nose stalls, tail stalls and axle stalls.

Switch

A stance where a rider puts their weaker foot in front. For a regular rider the right foot is in front. For a goofie rider the left foot is in front.

Tail

The end of the skate deck that is more curved inward. It is pointed behind the skater.

Tail skid

Stopping by hanging the heel off the edge of the board and throwing body weight on the back foot and tail of the board.

Team

A group of riders who represent a specific skateboard company.

Transition (or tranny)

What makes a ramp a ramp. The transition is the curved part of the ramp, between the coping and the flat bottom. It's the part you'll be riding up or down on.

Truck

The metal devices attached to the bottom of a skateboard. The trucks are what allow the skateboard to turn.

Varial flip

A trick that involves rotating the board from nose to tail and from top to bottom.

Wall

A skateboard obstacle that's just like any other wall.

Wallride

The act of skating up and on a wall.

Wheel

The four wheels that are attached to a skate deck.

Index